THE REAL
ALEXANDER
HAMILTON
THE TRUTH BEHIND THE LEGEND

by Jessica Gunderson

COMPASS POINT BOOKS
a capstone imprint

Real Revolutionaries is published by Compass Point Books,
1710 Roe Crest Drive, North Mankato, Minnesota 56003
www.capstonepub.com

Library of Congress Cataloging-in-Publication Data is on file with the Library of Congress.
Names: Gunderson, Jessica, author.
Title: The real Alexander Hamilton : the truth behind the legend / by Jessica Gunderson.
Description: North Mankato, Minnesota : Compass Point Books, [2019] |
Series: CPB grades 4-8. Real revolutionaries | Audience: Ages 10-14.
Identifiers: LCCN 2018042505| ISBN 9780756558925 (hardcover) |
ISBN 9780756561284 (paperback) | ISBN 9780756558970 (ebook pdf)
Subjects: LCSH: Hamilton, Alexander, 1757-1804—Juvenile literature. |
Statesmen—United States—Biography—Juvenile literature. | United States—Politics and
government—1783-1809—Juvenile literature.
Classification: LCC E302.6.H2 G86 2019 | DDC 973.4092—dc23
LC record available at https://lccn.loc.gov/2018042505

Editorial Credits
Nick Healy, editor; Sarah Bennett, designer; Eric Gohl, media researcher;
Kathy McColley, production specialist

Photo Credits
Alamy: Everett Collection Historical, 31, Ian Dagnall, cover, 1, M. Timothy O'Keefe, 8; Getty
Images: Bettmann, 25, Kean Collection, 53; Granger: 42; New York Public Library: 7, 11, 37, 39,
44; Newscom: Heritage Images/Historica Graphica Collection, 49; North Wind Picture Archives:
17, 19, 27; Wikimedia: Public Domain, 15, 57

Design Elements:
Shutterstock

Contents

CHAPTER ONE

AN EXTRAORDINARY LIFE 6

CHAPTER TWO

MYSTERIES AND MYTHS 26

CHAPTER THREE

THE UNKNOWN HAMILTON 34

CHAPTER FOUR

A FLAWED FIGURE 42

CHAPTER FIVE

A LASTING LEGACY 51

TIMELINE 58
GLOSSARY 60
FURTHER READING 61
SELECT BIBLIOGRAPHY 61
SOURCE NOTES 62
INDEX 64

AN EXTRAORDINARY LIFE

*F*or many years, Alexander Hamilton's face has been a familiar sight to Americans. After all, it has graced the ten-dollar bill for nearly a century. But in recent years, a hugely popular Broadway show—*Hamilton*—has made Alexander Hamilton a sort of modern celebrity. The story of Hamilton's rise and fall, told in hip-hop songs, brings this founding father to life in a memorable way. A likeness of Hamilton—one hand raised high—appears on top of a star in advertisements for the hit musical. In a few short years, this version of him has become another familiar sight in American culture.

Before the play inspired new interest in Hamilton, perhaps the best-known fact about Hamilton's life was how it ended. When studying history of the Revolutionary War era, many Americans learn about the famous duel that left Hamilton with a fatal wound.

But what else do people know about him? Why is he a historical figure who so fascinates Americans today?

Alexander Hamilton was the youngest of the United States' founding fathers. He helped draft the U.S. Constitution, and he wrote a series of essays to persuade the new nation to accept the Constitution as the law of the land. He served as the nation's first secretary of the treasury, and he promoted many of the economic principles that the United States still follows today. He was accomplished, brilliant, and controversial. And he came from a background quite unlike the other founding fathers.

A HUMBLE START IN LIFE

Alexander Hamilton was born on the Caribbean island of Nevis in 1755. The island was part of the British West Indies, territories of the British Empire. Nevis was a tropical paradise—blue skies, lush green hills, white beaches, and sea-green waves. It was a place far removed from the American colonial cities of Boston and

Philadelphia, with their cobblestone streets and clapboard houses, where several other founding fathers grew up.

Alexander's parents were not married. In fact, his mother, Rachel Fawcett Levien, was married to someone else. She had been separated from that man for a long time, but divorce was uncommon in those days and difficult to obtain. Alexander's father, James Hamilton, was a bit of a drifter. He couldn't settle down for long. He worked as a merchant, but he had a terrible sense for business. He never made much money.

James and Rachel couldn't get married legally, but they pretended they were married. James routinely introduced Rachel as his wife. The couple drifted from island to island in the Caribbean, as James tried to make

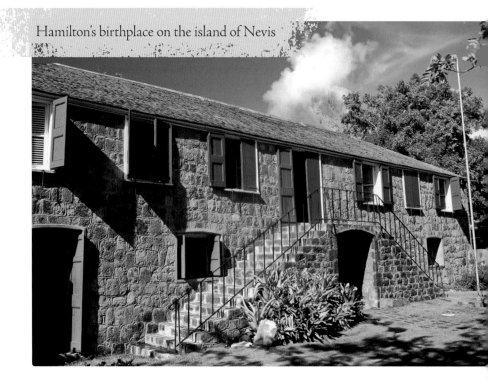

Hamilton's birthplace on the island of Nevis

a living. They had their first son, James Jr., in 1753. Two years later, Alexander was born. Rachel believed strongly in education, but her sons weren't allowed to attend the island schools because they were illegitimate, meaning their parents weren't married. Rachel hired private tutors for Alexander and his brother. And for a time, Alexander attended a small Jewish school on the island of Nevis, which allowed him in despite his parentage.

In 1765, when Alexander was 10 years old, his father abandoned the family. He left them in poverty. His abandonment left a wound in Alexander that never fully healed. To support her family, Rachel opened her own store on the island of St. Croix. The store sold goods to ship captains and local planters. Alexander went to work as a clerk at a business named Beekman and Cruger. He was a fast learner. He kept track of expenses and profits. But soon tragedy struck. Yellow fever spread through the island in 1768. Rachel fell ill and died. Just 13 years old, Alexander had lost his mother and been abandoned by his father.

Alexander and James Jr. went to live with a relative, Peter Lytton. But, unfortunately, Lytton soon died too. This event separated the brothers. James began an apprenticeship with a carpenter. Alexander went to live with a merchant named Thomas Stevens. He continued his work at Beekman and Cruger, learning the ins and outs of business. He even managed the business for several months, at the young age of 16, when his boss was ill.

Alexander spent his free time reading any book he could find. He also started writing his own poems and essays. When he was about 17, he published a poem in the local newspaper, the *Royal Danish American Gazette*.

In August 1772, the island of St. Croix was hit by a hurricane. Wild winds blew. Waves lashed the island. The storm tore ships from their moorings and splintered them to pieces. It uprooted crops and damaged structures. The island was left in shambles.

Days after the terrible storm, Alexander wrote a vivid description of the hurricane. He also included thoughtful insights about the storm's wrath and how he had thought about his own mortality in the frightening, violent circumstances. The description ended up being published in a local newspaper, and the community of St. Croix stood in awe of the teenager and his intelligence. A man named Hugh Knox took a special interest in the young man. He wanted to help Alexander receive an education, but his motives were not entirely selfless. Knox believed that the young man, with his sharp mind, could become a doctor—something the island needed.

Knox began raising funds to send Alexander to the American colonies for his education. In October 1772, Alexander boarded a ship bound for the American colonies. Despite the hopes and wishes of Hugh Knox, Hamilton would never to return to the islands of his youth.

CLOSE TO POWER

After only a few years in the American colonies, Hamilton had risen to unexpected heights. He became General George Washington's right-hand man. He surpassed the ranks of others who were older and more experienced than he was. How did Hamilton win the confidence of Washington, one of the colonies' most admired men? He did it by showing intelligence and skill at a crucial time in history.

Hamilton was 18 years old when he arrived in New York City in 1772. He enrolled in King's College, now Columbia University, in 1773. The tension between Great Britain and the American colonies was growing. In the 1760s, the British had begun imposing taxes on the colonists. The colonists had no representatives to vote on these tax laws. Many colonists felt the taxes were unfair. The cry of "No taxation without representation" rang out.

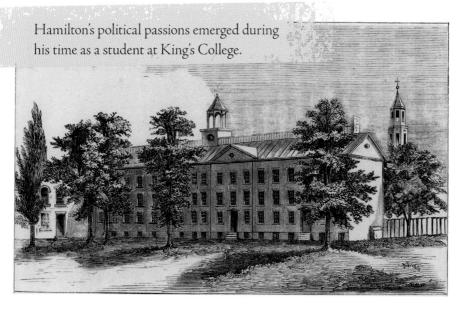

Hamilton's political passions emerged during his time as a student at King's College.

A group called the Sons of Liberty formed to protest unfair taxes and laws. In 1773, the British government passed the Tea Act. The Tea Act forced colonists to pay a high tax on all tea, except for tea from the British East India Company, which was struggling financially. The Tea Act favored the British company but hurt local tea importers in the colonies. To many colonists, the Tea Act was another example of taxation without representation. The enraged Sons of Liberty disguised themselves as Mowhawk Indians and stormed ships in the Boston Harbor. They dumped chests of tea into the harbor to show their dissatisfaction with the tea tax. This nighttime raid became known as the Boston Tea Party.

By that time, Alexander Hamilton, a college student, had taken a strong interest in politics. He agreed with the patriots in the Sons of Liberty and wrote several essays in 1774 and 1775. The unsigned essays were printed as pamphlets and advertised in the *New York Gazetteer* newspaper. Hamilton's essays showed great foresight, especially concerning the possibility of war with Great Britain. He wrote that the American militia would do better in battle in small wilderness skirmishes than in large, formal battles on open fields. He also wrote that Britain's enemies, particularly France, would aid the American cause. Both of these proved to be true when the war began.

In April 1775, shots rang out between American militia and British troops in what became known as the

Battles of Lexington and Concord. These battles marked the beginning of the Revolutionary War.

Hamilton loved learning, but he yearned to join the patriot effort. He dropped out of college and joined the Continental Army. Within a few months, he was appointed captain of an artillery unit. As the war continued, Hamilton's unit gained attention for its discipline and bravery. Other military leaders admired the young man, barely in his twenties, at its head. On November 29, 1776, a force of about 4,000 British and Hessian soldiers pursued General George Washington's army and arrived on the opposite bank of the Raritan River in New Jersey. The Americans quickly began destroying the bridge over the Raritan. Hamilton and his men unleashed a barrage of cannon fire at the British, holding them off until Washington and his men were safely away. At the Battle of Trenton on December 25, Hamilton and his men again cut down the Hessians with cannons. The Americans won the Battle of Trenton, a much-needed victory that boosted American confidence.

As a result of Hamilton's feats, General Washington asked him to be his aide-de-camp, which is an aide to a high-ranking officer. He also promoted Hamilton to lieutenant colonel. The two men developed a friendship that would last a lifetime.

As Washington's aide, Hamilton prepared reports for the general. He also wrote letters for him. Hamilton wrote to military leaders, members of Congress, and other officials. When France joined the war effort on the side of the Americans, Hamilton became even more valuable. He could speak French and was able to communicate effectively with French leaders in their own language.

Washington also sent Hamilton on military missions. In the fall of 1777, he consulted Hamilton on a military strategy to defeat the British. They were advancing toward Philadelphia, the patriot capital. As the British were about to capture Philadelphia in September 1777, Washington sent Hamilton inside the city to get ammunition, cannons, blankets, and other supplies.

After the British successfully took Philadelphia in September, Washington decided to launch an attack on British soldiers stationed at Germantown, just outside of Philadelphia. In the Battle of Germantown, in October 1777, a force of British soldiers inside a stone mansion fired on advancing American troops. Hamilton urged Washington to surround the house with a regiment to keep the British from escaping and then send the rest of the American army forward to continue attacking British soldiers on the ground. But Washington ignored Hamilton's advice. Instead, he followed artillery captain Henry Knox's advice to fire cannons at the house. The cannons did little damage, though, and the British sent deadly fire from inside the house, killing many American soldiers. The Americans retreated, and Germantown was a British victory. After this loss, Washington asked Hamilton to secure reinforcements from General Horatio

Gates. Hamilton rode north 150 miles (241 kilometers) to reach Gates. At first Gates refused, but eventually Hamilton persuaded him to send reinforcements.

Hamilton's travels took a toll on him, and he became ill for several weeks. In January 1778, after he recovered, Hamilton rejoined Washington's army at their winter camp in Valley Forge, Pennsylvania. Hamilton was shocked at what he found. The men were freezing and starving. Hamilton wrote a long letter to Congress that convinced them to send supplies and more troops.

In 1781, after leaving his job as Washington's aide-de-camp, Hamilton commanded a unit in the Battle of Yorktown. At Yorktown, Hamilton led 400 soldiers in an assault on a fortified British position. The Americans stormed through the British defenses and captured most of the enemy garrison positioned there. Hamilton's success was part of a larger triumph at Yorktown.

Hamilton led an assault on Redoubt 10, a steep-sided fortification that was an important part of British defenses at Yorktown.

British General Charles Cornwallis surrendered, and Yorktown became the last major land battle of the war. Afterward, the British government began negotiating an end to the war. Hamilton had been a key player in the Revolutionary War, and he was only a young man.

CREATING A GOVERNMENT

Hamilton also played a large role in forming the new government of the United States. During and after the war, the young country was governed by a set of laws called the Articles of Confederation. The articles had many flaws. One major problem was that states were only loosely connected. The central government had little power.

In September 1786, a group of representatives, including Hamilton, met in Annapolis, Maryland, to consider changes to the government. Hamilton pushed to replace the Articles of Confederation with something new. Some of the other representatives agreed. Hamilton wrote a letter to Congress calling for a national meeting to improve or replace the Articles of Confederation.

In May 1787, representatives from 12 of the 13 states gathered in Philadelphia for what would become known as the Constitutional Convention. (Rhode Island boycotted the convention, believing the convention would not be in the state's best interests.) Alexander Hamilton was a New York delegate to the convention. Early in the

The future of American government was a hot topic of conversation for Hamilton (right), Benjamin Franklin (left), and others in Philadelphia for the Constitutional Convention.

meeting, the delegates agreed to scrap the old Articles of Confederation and create a new plan of government. Two major plans—the Virginia Plan and the New Jersey Plan—were proposed. The Virginia Plan favored large states, whereas the New Jersey Plan gave equal power to small states. Hamilton didn't like either option.

On June 18, Hamilton presented his own plan. He proposed lifelong terms for the president and senators. He also mentioned getting rid of state governments entirely. Hamilton's plan was too extreme for most members of the convention, and it was dismissed. On June 30, Hamilton left the convention briefly to attend to personal business, and by July 6, the two other New York delegates had left for good. This meant that Hamilton's vote would hold no weight, since New York was no longer officially part of the convention. So Hamilton didn't return as planned. George Washington wrote him a letter, urging him to come back. Hamilton agreed and returned to Philadelphia.

A committee of delegates, known as the Great Committee, agreed upon a compromise between the Virginia Plan and the New Jersey Plan. On July 16, the Convention members voted to accept the compromise. Another committee then drafted the U.S. Constitution, which outlined the compromise. The Constitution proposed three branches of government—legislative, executive, and judicial. The legislative branch would be made up of representatives from each state, the executive branch would be made up of a president and the president's administration, and the judicial branch would be the Supreme Court. Each branch would balance out each other's power. Although the plan laid out in the Constitution was different from Hamilton's original proposal, it created the strong central government Hamilton wanted. The Constitution also contained some elements that were part of Hamilton's original plan, such as electing a single president rather than a presidential group, and having a federal Supreme Court to ensure that laws were constitutional. Although Hamilton wasn't fully pleased with the final plan, he was ready to support it.

Hamilton was appointed to the Committee of Style and Arrangement, which fine-tuned the language of the document. On September 17, after nearly four months of debate, the Constitution was finalized. Hamilton, along with 38 other delegates, signed the document. But the Constitution still had to be accepted by at least nine of the 13 states in order to become law. To make this happen, Hamilton created one of his crowning achievements, *The Federalist Papers.*

Hamilton knew the public needed to be convinced to accept the Constitution. And what better way to convince them than with his eloquent writing? He asked two other men, John Jay and James Madison, to join him in writing articles that supported the Constitution. These articles became known as *The Federalist Papers.*

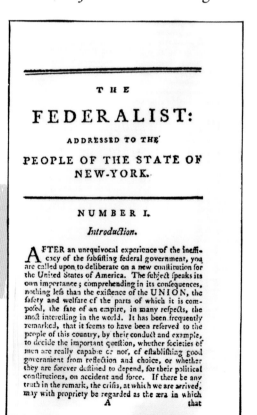

The Federalist, also known as *The Federalist Papers,* provided thoughtful arguments in support of the Constitution.

There were 85 articles altogether, published in various New York newspapers. Hamilton wrote 51 of the articles, He assured the public that the three branches of government would be balanced. Another important argument he made was that the Supreme Court would make sure all laws followed the Constitution. This would keep the government from passing unfair or punitive laws. Hamilton didn't sign his own name, though. He signed the articles as Publius after an ancient Roman hero.

One by one, the states began accepting the Constitution. When nine states had approved, or ratified, the Constitution, it became law on June 21, 1788. Hamilton's *Federalist Papers* played a large part in convincing the nation to accept the laws.

With the Constitution in place, Washington became the first president and soon looked to his former aide to fill an important job. He selected Hamilton to be part of his cabinet as the head of the Treasury Department. Hamilton became the first person to hold the role of U.S. Secretary of the Treasury.

Applying his good financial sense, Hamilton proposed a series of taxes. Funds from the taxes would help pay the nation's war debt. He also proposed creating a national bank called the Bank of the United States. The bank would hold the nation's funds, issue paper money, and help the nation build its credit. The government could borrow money from the bank when it needed to. President Washington signed the bank into existence in 1791.

AN OPPONENT OF SLAVERY

Hamilton's relative youth and upbringing set him apart from the other founding fathers in obvious ways. He also understood and viewed the world differently. This showed in his opposition to slavery in the United States.

Growing up in the Caribbean, Hamilton saw slavery firsthand. His mother even owned some enslaved people. In the Caribbean islands, there were 12 times more slaves than free citizens. The wealthy white plantation owners rode around in beautiful carriages and lived in fine homes. The enslaved people, on the other hand, toiled in the sugarcane fields and had horrible living conditions. They worked for no pay, and their lives were ruled by the whims of slaveholders.

Slavery in the United States traced back to a time long before the colonies fought for independence. Black people who were enslaved in the American colonies had been kidnapped from Africa by white people. They were transported across the ocean and sold to colonists. Then slave-owning white people forced them to work under brutal conditions on plantations, in homes, and at seaports. Enslaved people received no pay and had no rights. They were considered legal property, not human beings.

As an adult living in the U.S., Hamilton spoke out against slavery. He stated that slavery was inconsistent with America's ideals of freedom and equality. Hamilton tried to persuade the New York state legislature to buy slaves so they could be freed, but he didn't succeed. In 1785, Hamilton and a group of other New Yorkers organized the Society for Manumission of Slaves. The word "manumission" means to free one's slaves. Hamilton's society pushed to make slavery illegal in New York.

Hamilton also started a registry of freed slaves. Having their names on this list proved they were free. That way, they could not be forced back into slavery.

Although slavery in the United States would exist into the 1860s, when the Civil War finally settled the issue, Hamilton helped end slavery in New York state. The state eventually passed a law in 1799 that called for a gradual ban on slavery. In 1827, all slaves there were finally freed.

DEATH BY DUEL

Perhaps the most famous fact about Alexander Hamilton is the manner of his death—which followed a duel with rival politician Aaron Burr. Hamilton and Burr had a long-standing rivalry. Burr served as vice president under Thomas Jefferson. In 1800, Hamilton worked to prevent Burr's election as president. In 1804, Hamilton helped defeat Burr's bid to become the governor of New York. Hamilton described Burr as "a man of irregular and insatiable ambition [...] who ought not to be trusted with the reins of government."

When Burr heard what Hamilton said about him, he was furious. He sent a messenger to Hamilton, demanding an apology. When Hamilton wouldn't apologize, Burr formally challenged him to a duel.

Dueling was illegal in New York, but it had long been a way for gentlemen to defend their honor and settle disagreements. What exactly was a duel? Two men would agree to meet at a certain location at a certain time. Each man would bring a weapon, most commonly a pistol. And each man would have a "second"—a helper. The duelers were required to stand back-to-back before taking 10 paces, turning around, and firing after the supervising second yelled, "Present!" The person with the quicker hands and truer aim would win, and the other person would suffer the ultimate defeat. But often the duelers didn't actually want to kill each other. Instead, they would shoot to miss. And by participating in a duel, they showed they were willing to die to defend their honor.

Hamilton was no stranger to duels. His son Philip had been killed in a duel in 1801. As the story goes, Philip was angry over comments made in a speech by a young lawyer named George Eacker. In his speech, Eacker had attacked Alexander Hamilton. When Philip ran into Eacker at a theater, the two men argued. Neither would apologize, and a duel was arranged at Weehawken, New Jersey. At the dueling grounds, neither man fired for several moments. Then Eacker lifted his pistol and shot Philip. The younger Hamilton died a day later.

Fast forward three years to 1804. Even though his own son had been killed in a duel, Hamilton accepted Burr's challenge. Hamilton and Burr agreed to meet on July 11, 1804, at Weehawken, New Jersey—the very same place Philip had been fatally wounded.

Just before dawn on July 11, Hamilton rowed across the river to Weehawken, with his second, Nathaniel Pendleton, and his doctor, David Hosack. Burr was already there, waiting for his enemy.

Pendleton and Burr's second, William Van Ness, drew lots to determine who would supervise the event. Pendleton won. The seconds loaded the pistols and handed them to the duelers. The two men took their assigned places 10 paces apart. Pendleton asked if they were ready. Both Hamilton and Burr answered yes. Then Pendleton called, "Present!" Hamilton intentionally aimed away from Burr and shot a tree instead. But Burr shot Hamilton squarely in the abdomen.

Hamilton fell to the ground. Dr. Hosack rushed to him. "This is a mortal wound, Doctor," Hamilton whispered. But he still clung to life. Hosack and Pendleton lifted him into the boat and rowed him back to New York City to a friend's house. Hamilton lived for one more day. He died on July 12, 1804, with his wife, Elizabeth, at his bedside.

Aaron Burr, who was vice president at the time, shot Hamilton after years of bitterness between the two men. Burr was later charged with murder but was never convicted.

CHAPTER TWO

MYSTERIES AND MYTHS

*T*oday Alexander Hamilton seems to be a romantic figure. He was an abandoned and orphaned child from a tropical paradise. He was a young genius who became one of the nation's founding fathers, and he was killed in a duel. Certainly his life stands out when compared to the other founding fathers' lives. But a bit of mystery and myth surrounds him. Not all of what people think they know about him is true. Some often-repeated stories are myths that hide his true character.

DIVIDED LEADERS

One myth surrounding the founding fathers is that they all got along, happily forming the foundation of a new country promising life, liberty, and the pursuit of happiness. That's not exactly true. The founding fathers worked to create a unified country, but some of their relationships were difficult and tense. Angry quarrels erupted between them. And the most hot-headed and angry among them was Alexander Hamilton. He caused many of the disagreements.

As noted earlier, Hamilton and George Washington were friends and political allies. But even their friendship could be stormy. During the Revolutionary War, when Hamilton served as Washington's aide, the general trusted the young man. Though barely in his twenties, Hamilton handled many important documents and missions. He was a loyal aide. But in February 1781, the two men had a falling out.

Washington (left) and Hamilton (right) were closely linked, but the two had quite different personalities.

Hamilton was on his way to deliver a letter when he passed Washington on the stairs. Washington asked to speak with Hamilton. Hamilton told him he had to deliver the letter first. When Hamilton returned, Washington accused him of being disrespectful and keeping him waiting. Hamilton, angered, replied: "I am not conscious of it, sir; but since you have thought it necessary to tell me, so we part." And then Hamilton resigned.

Washington tried to patch things up, but Hamilton refused. Hamilton later said that he had "felt no friendship" for Washington for three years and was tired of being at his beck and call. After some time passed, the two became friends again, but the rift never fully mended.

The feud with Washington was not Hamilton's last with a powerful figure. He bickered with the governor of New York, George Clinton. He accused Clinton of profiting personally from his policies. The two men were at odds for many years. When Hamilton became the secretary of the treasury, Thomas Jefferson, who was secretary of state, and John Adams, the vice president, disliked Hamilton so much they tried to get rid of him.

But Hamilton endured. With his fiery personality, he never backed down from quarrels with his fellow patriots.

HAMILTON'S COMPLAINTS

Another myth surrounding Hamilton is that he was a staunch patriot from the very beginning of the war.

It's true that he supported American independence and left college to fight in the Revolutionary War. But, as the war went on, Hamilton expressed a desire to leave the country. He wrote to his childhood friend, "I am a stranger in this country. I have no property here, no connections." He added, "I wish to make a brilliant exit."

He was disgusted by the Continental Congress, and he believed it was Congress' fault the war was dragging on. At one point he wrote, "I hate Congress–I hate the army." He also thought Americans were lazy, and that, "We labor less now than any civilized nation of Europe."

Why did he write such angry thoughts? He was angry with the way the war was going. He was also frustrated because he wanted a combat position rather than an aide position with Washington. By the war's end, though, Hamilton had become a devoted patriot again. He never again said he wanted to leave the country.

AN IMMIGRANT AGAINST IMMIGRANTS?

One long-standing myth is that Hamilton was a strong supporter of open immigration—accepting immigrants no matter where they are from. As an immigrant himself, Hamilton might have favored open doors for others like him. But he didn't—at least not completely. He was a bit of a flip-flopper on immigration.

Hamilton supported some policies that opened the door for immigrants. Those were mostly policies that would help the United States financially. In his 1791 *Report on Manufactures*, he wrote that manufacturing would bring immigrants to the country. This would help the United States' population to grow.

He also argued against one aspect of the Constitution that concerns immigrants serving in Congress. The Constitution requires that people serving in Congress must be born in the United States, or if not, they must have lived in the U.S. for a number of years. A U.S. Senator must have been a U.S. citizen for at least nine years, and a U.S. Representative must have been a citizen for at least seven years. Hamilton argued that this citizenship rule would keep wealthy immigrants from coming to the United States.

While he was interested in protecting the rights of immigrants when it could benefit the country, he also supported anti-immigration policies. The harshest anti-immigration policies he supported were included in the Alien and Sedition Acts of 1798.

The Alien and Sedition Acts were four bills signed into law by President John Adams in 1798. One of these bills, the Naturalization Act, made it harder for an immigrant to become a citizen. Before the bill, immigrants had to be a resident of the United States for five years before they could become U.S. citizens. The Naturalization Act increased this period to 14 years. Immigrants also had to declare that they wanted to be a citizen, and then wait five years before becoming one.

By the President of the United States of America.

A Proclamation.

WHEREAS by an act of the Congress of the United States, passed the ninth day of February last, entitled, "An act further to suspend the commercial intercourse between the United States and France, and the dependencies thereof," it is provided, That at any time after the passing of this act, it shall be lawful for the President of the United States, if he shall deem it expedient and consistent with the interests of the United States by his order, to remit and discontinue for the time being, the restraints and prohibitions by the said act imposed, either with respect to the French Republic, or to any island, port or place, belonging to the said Republic, with which a commercial intercourse may safely be renewed ; and also to revoke such order, whenever in his opinion the interest of the United States shall require : and he is authorised to make proclamation thereof accordingly.

And whereas the arrangements which have been made at St. Domingo for the safety of the commerce of the United States, and for the admission of American vessels into certain ports of that island, do in my opinion, render it expedient and for the interest of the United States to renew a commercial intercourse with such ports.

Therefore I JOHN ADAMS, President of the United States, by virtue of the powers vested in me by the aforesaid act, do hereby remit and discontinue the restraints and prohibitions therein contained, within the limits and under the regulations here following, to wit :

1. It shall be lawful for vessels which have departed or may depart from the United States, to enter the ports of Cape Francois, and Port Republican, formerly called Port au Prince, in the said island of St. Domingo, on and after the first day of August next.

2. No vessel shall be cleared for any other port in St. Domingo, than Cape Francois and Port Republicain.

3. It shall be lawful for vessels which shall enter the said ports of Cape Francois and Port Republicain, after the thirty-first day of July next, to depart from thence to any other port in said island between Monte Christi on the North, and Petit Goave on the West ; provided it be done with the consent of the government of St. Domingo, and pursuant to certificates or passports expressing such consent, signed by the consul-general of the United States, or consul residing at the port of departure.

4. All vessels failing in contravention of these regulations, will be out of the protection of the United States, and be moreover liable to capture, seizure, and confiscation.

(L. S.) Given under my hand and the seal of the United States, at Philadelphia, the twenty-sixth day of June, in the year of our Lord 1799, and of the Independence of the said States, the twenty-third.

JOHN ADAMS.

By the President.

TIMOTHY PICKERING, Secretary of State.

Extract of a letter from ROBERT LISTON, Esq. Minister Plenipotentiary of his Britannic Majesty to the United States, dated New-York, July 13, 1799, to his Excellency Vice Admiral Sir HYDE PARKER.

"I have just learnt with concern, by a letter from Brigadier General Maitland, dated at Sea, (lat. 35, N. long. 68, W.) the 2d of this month, that there has been a misunderstanding on the subject of the time fixed for renewing the commercial intercourse between the United States and St. Domingo.

"In the agreement entered into by General Maitland and myself with the American ministers, it was clearly understood by all parties and fixed,—that the stipulated ports in the island should be opened on a certain day for the reception of the merchant vessels of Great Britain and the United States ; NOT that the ports of America and of Jamaica should be opened on a certain day. In consequence of this understanding, and the subsequent arrangements between General Maitland and the American Consul General in St. Domingo, the President has by a Proclamation dated the 26th of June, informed the inhabitants of this country, that it shall be lawful for vessels, which have departed or may depart from the United States, to enter the ports of Cape François and Port-au-Prince on or after the first of August next.

"Dr. Stevens, it seems, now conceives the meaning of the agreement to have been that vessels should not clear out from the American States till the 1st of August ; and General Maitland informs me, that you have given orders to your cruisers accordingly.

"It is impossible however, considering the time that has elapsed and the extent of the territory of the United States, that the President should now make any alteration in the measures adopted (we're it decorous that he should do so ;) indeed many vessels have already sailed, and are daily sailing from the different American ports, with a view to be ready to enter into Cape François and Port-au-Prince on the day appointed.

"I take the first opportunity of mentioning this embarrassing circumstance, regretting that it was not in my power to give you the information sooner ; and it remains that I should entreat you to be pleased without loss of time to take such measures, in concert with Dr. Stevens and his Majesty's Lieutenant Governor of Jamaica, as may be calculated to effect the opening of the ports in question with the least possible delay ; and I trust that you will at the same time have the goodness to give such orders to your cruisers as will ensure to the American vessels, which have thus left their ports without any view to a fraudulent commerce, and by the express permission of their government, every necessary attention and good treatment."

I TIMOTHY PICKERING, Secretary for the Department of State of the United States of America, hereby certify, That the foregoing Proclamation is a true copy of the original remaining in my office, and that the foregoing extract is faithfully copied from an original letter to Sir Hyde Parker, sent to me under a flying seal by Mr. Liston for my information : Given under my hand and official seal, at Philadelphia, this 17th day of July A. D. 1799.

Timothy Pickering

The Alien and Sedition Acts, a group of four laws, increased burdens on immigrants and restricted speech critical of the government.

Also, only white people could become citizens.

Another of these bills was the Alien Friends Act. This bill allowed the president to imprison or deport any noncitizen who was considered dangerous. Another act, the Alien Enemies Act, allowed the president to deport any noncitizen who was from a "hostile nation"—in other words, a nation at war with the United States. The fourth act was the Sedition Act, which made it illegal to speak out against the government or the president.

Clearly, the Alien and Sedition Acts were against immigrants. So why would Alexander Hamilton support such laws? One major reason was that recent immigrants largely supported the opposing political party, the Democratic-Republicans. Another reason was that Federalists feared a war with France. France and Great Britain were at war, and the U.S. government had signed the Jay Treaty with Great Britain, which angered the French. The Alien Friends Act and the Alien Enemies Act were targeted toward French immigrants or those who supported France.

In 1801, Thomas Jefferson, a Democratic-Republican, became president and wanted to do away with the Alien and Sedition Acts. In his first message to Congress, Jefferson spoke about the benefits of immigration.

Hamilton held an opposing viewpoint. Despite his own background as an immigrant, he was suspicious of immigrants. He wrote that immigrants remain deeply attached to their birth countries. And this was dangerous, in Hamilton's view. He wrote that "the influx of foreigners" would "change and corrupt the national spirit." He also wrote that the "United States have already felt the evils of incorporating a large number of foreigners into their national mass."

A CAT NAMED HAMILTON

There once was a cat named Hamilton. Or was there? As the story goes, First Lady Martha Washington named her cat Hamilton. Why? Because the cat loved his female friends. And Hamilton, too, liked to flirt with ladies. This story has been told many times by various historians. In the popular musical *Hamilton*, the character of Aaron Burr sings about it. And in the musical, Hamilton agrees with this perception of his character.

But is it true? No one knows for sure. Some historians say that the rumor may have been started by John Adams, Hamilton's political enemy. Others believe the story started with a tongue-in-cheek newspaper article published in 1780 that states, "Mrs. Washington has a mottled tom-cat (which she calls, in a complimentary way, 'Hamilton')."

The article never mentioned anything about the cat's affection for ladies or why Martha named him after Hamilton. So, if Martha Washington named her cat Hamilton, it seems to be out of respect, rather than a comment about his flirtatiousness.

It can't be proven one way or another. But the myth about Hamilton the cat persists to this day.

CHAPTER THREE

THE UNKNOWN HAMILTON

Alexander Hamilton had a lasting impact on the United States, but for many years his star had dimmed. Many Americans knew little about him and what he stood for. The success of the Broadway musical bearing Hamilton's name has changed that. He is a household name, and his life has been explored in a stream of news articles, books, and television shows. To some people, Hamilton may seem a familiar figure, but still there are many aspects of his life that few Americans know about.

FOILING BENEDICT ARNOLD

One interesting story about Hamilton features another noteworthy figure from the Revolutionary War, Benedict Arnold. During the Revolutionary War, Arnold was a skilled American general in the Continental Army.

He led his forces to key victories over the British. His capture of Fort Ticonderoga, New York, in 1775 was a crucial moment in the war. He also held off British troops at the Battle of Valcour Island, giving the American army time to prepare. And he fought courageously at the Battle of Saratoga in 1777.

But in the end, he turned against the American cause. He asked to command West Point, a key fort in New York. Then he communicated secretly with the British, giving them inside information about the fort and the Americans' strategy.

Alexander Hamilton was an eyewitness to Arnold's betrayal. In September 1780, General Washington decided to stop at West Point and see Benedict Arnold. He sent Hamilton and another aide ahead to prepare Arnold's headquarters for his arrival. On the morning of September 25, Hamilton was having breakfast with Arnold. A messenger burst into the room and told Arnold that a spy referred to as John Anderson had been caught. In his boot, the spy had hidden detailed descriptions of West Point. As the messenger told Arnold about it, Hamilton noticed Arnold's nervousness. Arnold hopped to his feet, raced from the room, and slipped away from the house.

Washington showed up soon thereafter and was surprised that Arnold had left so quickly. He went on to inspect West Point's fort. He didn't suspect Arnold of treason. Hamilton stayed at Arnold's headquarters to sort through some papers. When Washington returned, Hamilton gave him a packet of dispatches, including the papers found on the spy called John Anderson. The papers clearly incriminated Benedict Arnold. Washington burst out, "Arnold has betrayed us!"

Washington sent Hamilton to chase after Arnold. Hamilton leaped onto his horse and raced along the river. He knew Arnold was heading across British lines. Hamilton rode for miles as fast as he could, but he was too late. Before Hamilton could catch up, Arnold had boarded the British ship *Vulture*.

Immediately, Hamilton took charge of the situation. He knew that West Point was in danger. He sent a message to General Nathanael Greene, calling for backup troops. He wrote that there had been "a scene of the blackest treason" and that the general should march "immediately this way."

The captured spy called John Anderson was, in fact, a British officer named John André. Washington organized a board of officers to determine the spy's fate. The board found him guilty of spying and sentenced him to death by hanging. Hamilton, though, felt sympathy for André. André was an old friend of Hamilton's fiancée, Elizabeth Schuyler, and he may have argued on André's behalf in order to please her. He also admired André, writing that he wished he was "possessed of André's accomplishments" and that André had a "peculiar elegance of mind and manners."

A crowd gathered to watch as John André was taken to his execution.

Hamilton visited him in his cell several times, and he told Washington that André should be shot like a gentleman rather than hanged like a common criminal. But Washington refused. André was hanged a week later, and Hamilton was in the crowd.

WRITING WASHINGTON'S FAREWELL

One of President George Washington's most famous works was his farewell address, which he published at the end of his presidency. For more than 60 years, most people thought Washington wrote the address. But in 1854, Hamilton's wife, Elizabeth, died, and in 1859, Hamilton's papers were released. The papers revealed something surprising. Hamilton, not Washington, had written much of the Farewell Address.

During George Washington's presidency, there were no term limits. In other words, people could serve as president for as many times as they were elected. In fact, most people expected Washington to serve for life. Hamilton himself, during the Constitutional Convention, had pushed for a president who served for life.

In 1792, at the end of his first term, Washington debated stepping down. He asked James Madison to write a farewell speech for him. Madison drafted a speech, but Washington decided to serve another term.

By the end of his second term, Washington knew it was time to step down. He made the decision not to run for a third term for several reasons. He thought it would be unfair and selfish for him to serve any longer. He also wanted to retire. Another important reason was the nation's divided party politics. When Washington became president, there were no political parties, but by the end of his second term, there were two—the Federalists and the Democratic-Republicans. Washington was a Federalist, and he was convinced he wouldn't get any votes from the other party.

The president believed he should explain to the American people why he was stepping down. He knew that many Americans feared what might happen to the young country without him as their leader. To get his message across, Washington turned to his old friend Hamilton. The president wanted to describe his ideas in a way that would be understood. Hamilton had always had a magical and elegant way with words. And by that time in their careers, the two men had similar ideas about politics and the role of the federal government.

Washington revised the 1792 Madison speech, adding some of his own points. He sent it to Hamilton, asking him to either revise the draft or write an entirely new one. Hamilton decided to do both. First, he wrote a new draft, using some of the ideas from the Madison-Washington draft. Then, he revised the speech Washington had sent him. Washington decided to use Hamilton's new draft with some of his own words added in. The farewell address called for unity of the country. It also explained that Washington was not the reason the United States became a strong country. Instead, he said in the address, the American citizens helped the country grow and prosper.

Hamilton's handwritten draft of President Washington's farewell address

The farewell address was first printed in a newspaper, and then it was published as a pamphlet and sold throughout the country. Only a few people knew that the main author was Hamilton.

One day, Hamilton and his wife Elizabeth were walking down Broadway in New York City. A man approached them, wanting to sell them a copy of the farewell address. Hamilton bought one. Then he turned to Elizabeth, laughed, and said, "That man does not know he has asked me to purchase my own work."

So why was Hamilton's authorship kept secret? Over the years presidential speechwriters usually have stayed in the background. They don't take credit for their work. They provide words to help explain the president's ideas. And even as the first president left office, that idea held sway. Most likely, Hamilton did not want to take away from Washington's success as president.

In 1862, Congress began a tradition of having a legislator read the farewell address aloud each year on Washington's birthday. Perhaps they should read it on Hamilton's birthday too.

ANOTHER DUEL?

Hamilton's death by duel is a well-known fact about him. But one little-known truth is that this wasn't the first time Hamilton had been challenged to a duel. In fact, he had come close to dueling nearly a dozen times.

One particular instance came in a 1797 dispute with James Monroe, who would become the fifth president of the United States (1817–1825). The trouble started when a journalist named James Callender published pamphlets tarnishing Hamilton's reputation. Hamilton believed Monroe had pushed Callender to publish the accusations. And he was angry. He wrote Monroe, saying the two should have an "interview" and bring "seconds."

Monroe didn't immediately respond, so Hamilton went to visit him. The two argued angrily.

"You're a scoundrel!" Monroe said.

"I will meet you like a gentleman," Hamilton retorted. His words were a veiled challenge to a duel.

"I am ready," Monroe spat. "Get your pistols."

The two men stared one another down, ready to punch. But others in the room pried them apart, telling them to calm down and discuss the matter. The issue wasn't totally resolved by the end of the meeting, and Hamilton and Monroe exchanged letters about it for a year afterward. Hamilton's letters always hinted at a duel, and Monroe said he would accept.

Then another man stepped in to calm the waters. He succeeded in convincing them not to duel. Who was this man? None other than Aaron Burr. It's a strange fact that if Burr hadn't stepped in, Hamilton might have been killed by another founding father, James Monroe.

CHAPTER FOUR

A FLAWED FIGURE

*A*lexander Hamilton was ambitious, and his ambition led him to great heights in his life. He went from being a homeless child to an educated leader in the founding of the United States. He went from being a young college student to General George Washington's right-hand man. And he went from being a private in the army to a major general while still a young man.

But Alexander Hamilton's nature also proved to be one of his downfalls. He often put his values aside in order to follow his ambition, even if it led him down a dark path.

A CLIMBER IN LIFE

Alexander Hamilton had always been driven, even as a young boy. He read and reread the books his mother kept in her attic. He wanted to be somebody who stood out, someone who made something of his life.

In 1770, when Hamilton was a teenager on the island of St. Croix, his best friend, Edward Stevens, moved far away. Edward was off to New York City to attend prep school. Then he was going on to King's College to become a doctor. Hamilton was jealous of his friend. At the time, Hamilton was working as a clerk at Beekman and Cruger, an export business. With his mother dead and his father gone, he didn't think he'd ever be able to go on to college.

Alexander wrote to his friend, saying he despised having to be a lowly clerk "to which my fortune condemns me." He knew there was most likely no way out, except for one thing. "I wish there was a war," Alexander wrote. He knew that a war would give him the opportunity to showcase his bravery and intelligence. And then, perhaps, he could rise through the ranks. This desire for war revealed a dark aspect of Hamilton's ambition. He dreamed of war, which would kill many people, just so he could fulfill his ambitions.

And Hamilton got his wish. The Revolutionary War broke out in 1775, and Hamilton climbed the ranks to become General Washington's aide. But by then, he was in New York enrolled at college when the war started. He might have become successful even without a war.

Hamilton's ambitions also led him to be something of a social climber. In other words, he tried to befriend the rich and powerful so he could advance himself. One of the main ways people climbed the social ladder was to marry someone of a higher class. So Hamilton set out to find a wife.

Hamilton wrote to his friend John Laurens that he wanted a wife who came from wealth. He wrote, "the larger stock of [fortune], the better." He went on to say that "money is an essential ingredient of happiness in this world." The letter was written with a bit of humor, but it conveyed what he wanted from a wife—wealth and status.

Hamilton courted a few young women, all of high social standing. Then, early in 1780, he met Elizabeth Schuyler. The Schuylers were one of the wealthiest and most powerful families in the United States. Hamilton fell head over heels for Elizabeth. The two exchanged love letters, and soon they were engaged.

Elizabeth Schuyler met Hamilton when he paid a visit to her aunt's home.

Some historians believe that Hamilton was drawn to Elizabeth because of her wealth and high-society connections. Marrying into the Schuyler family certainly helped Hamilton rise to the top of society.

The Schuylers gave the orphaned Hamilton a place in society. And Hamilton believed he had a right to this place. Even though he had been a penniless orphan, he'd come from a noble family line. His father, James, was the son of a Scottish lord and landowner. James had been raised in a castle called The Grange in Ayrshire, Scotland. As the fourth son, James knew he wouldn't inherit much of anything. The older sons would get the bulk of the wealth. So James went to the West Indies. Alexander Hamilton was proud of his family heritage. He even named his grand home in Manhattan "The Grange," after his ancestors' castle.

Hamilton's family background is one reason he believed the government should be an aristocracy. In an aristocracy, power in government and society is held by a small, privileged upper class of people. Although he believed in equality in many ways, Hamilton felt the government should be run by wealthy landowners, merchants, and the educated. He didn't trust the common people to make good decisions for the country. During the Constitutional Convention in 1787, he said, "The people are turbulent and changing; they seldom judge or determine right." He went on to say that the upper class should hold the power because the rich "will check the unsteadiness" of the common people. He also believed that senators and the president should serve for life. He even stated that the president should inherit the presidential role. In other words, he felt the presidency should be passed down through the family line, like royalty.

Hamilton's opponents attacked his ideas. They thought his form of government would be just like Great Britain's monarchy all over again. A president serving for life, and who inherited the position, would be just like a king. In the end, the founders chose a more moderate plan—James Madison's Virginia Plan—and applied it in the Constitution. Hamilton's aristocratic idea had been rejected. To his credit, he defended the Constitution fiercely, even though it didn't suit his original notions.

Hamilton's ambitions also caused him to put aside issues that were important to him. One of these issues was slavery. Since he was a youth on St. Croix island, Hamilton had hated slavery. As an adult in the United States, he became involved in antislavery organizations. But he also tended to ignore slavery when it benefited him.

One example was his friendship with George Washington. Washington owned more than 100 enslaved people, who worked in his home and on his plantation at Mount Vernon. Hamilton avoided talking about it, even though he despised slavery. And Hamilton's own in-laws—the Schuylers—owned several slaves.

When it came to building the foundation of the United States, Hamilton also put aside his distaste for slavery. He accepted that slaves were considered property under the Constitution. In *The Federalist Papers*, he defended property rights. He knew that the southern states might not accept the Constitution unless slavery was protected. Also, like many fellow founders, he recognized how much the South—with its plantations and enslaved labor force—helped the United States financially. So, ultimately, he accepted the Constitution with its protection of slavery. Only later in his life did he work to end slavery by forming the Manumission Society of New York.

THE FEUDING FOUNDER

Alexander Hamilton's fiery personality got him into a lot of trouble—and, in the end, got him killed. He was hotheaded, argumentative, opinionated, and somewhat snobbish. He didn't hold back from stating his opinions. He had many feuds with the other founding fathers, which led to political divisions even in the country's earliest days. His personality eventually became his downfall.

Hamilton didn't like the idea of political parties. No official political parties existed when the Constitution was written. Those who supported the Constitution were called Federalists, and those against it were Anti-Federalists. The Federalists won out, and George Washington became president with no opposition and no official party.

Both Hamilton and Washington believed in a strong national government. As secretary of the treasury, Hamilton was in favor of financial policies that supported a strong central government. As he worked to create the Bank of the United States, he knew he needed widespread support. He started building connections with powerful bankers, businessmen, and merchants. This group of people eventually became the nation's first political party, the Federalist Party, in 1791.

But two of the other founding fathers resisted Hamilton's policies. They were Thomas Jefferson, who was the secretary of state under President Washington, and James Madison. Jefferson and Madison favored states' rights over a strong central government. They also despised the idea of a central bank, believing it would favor the wealthy. In the early 1790s, they formed their own party, called the Democratic-Republican Party.

Jefferson was one of Hamilton's main political enemies. The two had very different ideas about the future of the United States. Hamilton wanted a strong federal government and an economy based on manufacturing and banking. Jefferson believed in strong state and local governments and wanted to protect an economy based on farming. The two men had very different personalities as well. Hamilton was outgoing and outspoken, while Jefferson was reserved and thoughtful. President Washington could sense the tension between the two men. He wrote them nearly identical letters, hinting

Founders (from left to right) John Adams, Gouverneur Morris, Alexander Hamilton, and Thomas Jefferson did not all share the same vision for the federal government.

that they should strive to get along. Although they remained political enemies, the two were able to work together in Washington's administration.

Another famous name among Hamilton's enemies was John Adams. Adams, who became the nation's second president in 1797, was a Federalist like Hamilton. But the two didn't like each other. When the French Revolution broke out, Adams knew he needed to build up his military in case the United States got involved. Washington told him to appoint Hamilton as the army's major general. Adams reluctantly agreed. But he limited Hamilton's power and eventually disbanded Hamilton's unit altogether. Hamilton's dislike of Adams grew. When Adams was up for reelection in 1800, Hamilton wanted to sabotage him.

Adams was running as a Federalist against two Democratic-Republican nominees, Thomas Jefferson and Aaron Burr. Hamilton didn't like any of them.

But he disliked Adams the most. Just before the election, Hamilton wrote a bitter attack on Adams, saying he was emotionally unstable and that Adams "is not fit to be president." He persuaded others in his party to vote for Charles Pinckney, another Federalist, instead.

In the end, Adams came in third. Thomas Jefferson and Aaron Burr, Democratic-Republicans, were tied for first. So now the House of Representatives had the deciding vote. The House of Representatives had a majority of Federalists, so the decision was in the hands of Hamilton's party.

Although Hamilton and Jefferson were political enemies, Hamilton favored Jefferson over Burr. But most Federalists wanted Burr to be president. Hamilton got to work and convinced several Federalist members of the House of Representatives to vote for Jefferson. He said Jefferson was "by far not so dangerous a man" as Burr. In the end, Jefferson won by a single vote, and Burr became vice president.

Hamilton's actions ended up bringing about the end of his own Federalist Party. The 1800 election had split the party between those loyal to Hamilton and those loyal to Adams. Members began to break off. Hamilton lost credibility, and his political career was over. By 1824, the Federalist Party had dissolved completely.

And with his support of Jefferson, Hamilton made another lasting enemy—Aaron Burr, an enemy who would later kill him.

CHAPTER FIVE

A LASTING LEGACY

*A*lexander Hamilton led an intriguing and exciting life. He was an abandoned child, a founding father, an author, and a bit of a troublemaker. Although his life was cut short, it was filled with accomplishments. His lasting achievement was building the financial foundation of the United States.

Hamilton had great business sense. It blossomed when he was just a teenager, working as a clerk for the export business of Beekman and Cruger. He was quick with numbers, and he understood the economy—the production, use, and sale of goods in a country.

In 1789, President George Washington created the U.S. Treasury Department to handle the nation's finances. He appointed Hamilton as the United States' first secretary of the treasury. The young nation was struggling financially. It had millions of dollars of debt as a result of the Revolutionary War. Hamilton knew that the United States had to pay its debts and strengthen its finances in order to survive. This would help establish credibility with other countries. But it wouldn't be easy. Hamilton faced a very tough task.

Hamilton's first idea was to raise taxes on goods imported from other countries. This would help the country pay its war debts as well as states' individual debts. Hamilton's plan was met with much disagreement, especially from Thomas Jefferson, secretary of state.

Some states, such as Jefferson's home state of Virginia, had already paid their war debts, and they didn't feel their residents should have to pay tariffs. Jefferson stated that he would support Hamilton's plan under one condition. He insisted that the nation's capital must move from New York City to Virginia. Hamilton believed strongly in his plan, so he compromised with Jefferson and the Virginia congressmen. The nation's capital moved to the banks of the Potomac River in northern Virginia, in what became the city of Washington, D.C.

Hamilton believed in a strong central government. And a strong central government needed the ability to borrow money when necessary. So he proposed an idea for a national bank—the Bank of the United States. It would be modeled after the Bank of England. The bank would hold the nation's money, offer banking facilities for commercial transactions, and allow the government to borrow money when needed.

Hamilton's idea was met with opposition. Some resisted the idea of modeling the bank after the Bank of England. They feared the United States would become too much like England, which the Americans had just fought to get away from. Additionally, people felt that a centralized bank put too much financial power in the hands of the federal government. Despite opposition, George Washington signed a law creating the bank in 1791.

The bank operated for 20 years, until Congress failed to renew the bank's charter. But the War of 1812 caused the nation to go into debt again. In 1816, the Second

The building that housed the First Bank of the United States was constructed in Philadelphia in 1795.

Bank of the United States went into effect, modeled after Hamilton's First Bank. The Second Bank was dissolved in 1836, and the United States was without a central bank for nearly 80 years. In 1913, President Woodrow Wilson signed the Federal Reserve Act, which set up a system of central public and private banks to help stabilize the nation's finances. Alexander Hamilton's vision laid the foundation for the central banking system the nation uses today.

One issue that troubled Hamilton was the lack of a strong U.S. dollar. During the Revolutionary War, the U.S. issued the Continental currency (printed money), which quickly lost value. Individual states also issued their own paper currencies. People were also using the Spanish peso to buy goods. Hamilton knew that the nation needed a sound currency to replace the Continentals and state-issued money. In 1791, he submitted a report to the House of Representatives, explaining the importance of establishing a U.S. Mint. The mint would produce U.S. coins that would be circulated. One aspect of his proposal was to produce small-value coins as well as those of larger values. He stated that minting small-value coins would help the poor, in part by allowing common people to get used to handling money. Congress agreed to his plan. The first U.S. Mint was established in Philadelphia in 1792. Today, there are four U.S. Mints that produce coins and paper money. The mints are in Philadelphia, Denver, San Francisco, and West Point, New York.

Hamilton also had a role in creating the U.S. Coast Guard. At the time, piracy and smuggling were problems on American coasts. Smugglers sneaked in goods from other countries to avoid paying duties or tariffs. Since tariffs were a major part of Hamilton's plan to fund the nation's debt, he knew smuggling was a problem the nation must address. He presented a plan to Congress for guard boats—called cutters—to patrol the coasts and intercept smuggled goods. This guard boat plan worked, and the force eventually became the U.S. Coast Guard, which still protects American coasts today.

Hamilton's most significant achievements as secretary of treasury had to do with increasing manufacturing in the United States. At the time, the country's economy centered on agriculture and a rural way of life. Hamilton believed manufacturing, or the production of goods, would make for a stronger foundation for the economy. In December 1791, he presented a report to Congress titled *Report on Manufactures*. The report relayed the importance of establishing factories and manufacturing facilities around the country.

Hamilton believed that manufacturing would help the nation become more independent. If the U.S. could produce its own goods for its citizens, it would not have to rely on other countries for goods and products. He also believed that manufacturing would provide many jobs for people of all backgrounds. It would also provide the common man with opportunities to be inventive, creative, and innovative. And manufacturing would also help the nation grow. With more jobs available, people would flock to the United States and increase its population.

Hamilton believed the U.S. government should be active in helping manufacturing grow. He wanted the government to provide funding to support factories and other manufacturing facilities.

Hamilton's ideas were bold. The U.S. economy was built on agriculture, not manufacturing. Many powerful people hoped to protect that way of life. Landowners, with their sweeping farms and plantations, held much of the wealth of the country. Among the nation's early leaders, Thomas Jefferson and James Madison resisted Hamilton's ideas. They were afraid he wanted to replace farming with manufacturing. They also disagreed with his idea that the U.S. government should fund the manufacturing industry. Hamilton argued that the two could coexist to create a strong economy.

In the end, the House of Representatives did not act on the *Report on Manufactures*. But Hamilton's ideas had a lasting impact. His ideas became the basis of The American School (or National System) of economics. This system promoted protectionism—in other words, protecting American manufacturing by taxing goods from other countries. It also promoted government funding of infrastructure, such as roads, waterways, and eventually railways, as well as a central bank.

The American
School ideas were
implemented in the
U.S. from the 1860s
through the 1970s.
During this time,
American industry
grew. By the end of
the 19th century, the
United States had
the largest economy
in the world.
Alexander Hamilton
didn't live to see
his ideas take hold,
but he had great
foresight regarding
the economic future
of the young nation.

As the first U.S. secretary of the treasury, Alexander
Hamilton established a national currency and a tax
system that helped the nation pay its war debt. His ideas
about manufacturing and economic independence fueled
future growth of the American manufacturing industry.
In recognition of his achievements, Hamilton stares back
at Americans from every ten-dollar bill.

TIMELINE

JANUARY 1755
Alexander Hamilton is born on the island of Nevis
in the Caribbean.

1765
Alexander Hamilton's father, James, leaves the family.

1765
Great Britain passes the Stamp Act, requiring American
colonists to place a paid stamp on all printed documents.
This act angers colonists who had no say in the law.

1768
James's mother, Rachel, dies.

AUGUST 1772
A devastating hurricane strikes the island of St. Croix.
Hamilton writes a description of the destruction
which showcases his intelligence.

OCTOBER 1772
Hamilton leaves the Caribbean for the American colonies.

1773
Hamilton enrolls in Kings College, New York.

1775
The Revolutionary War begins with the Battles of Lexington
and Concord. Hamilton leaves college to fight in the war.

1777
Hamilton becomes General George Washington's aide.

1780
Hamilton marries Elizabeth Schuyler.

1781
Hamilton leaves Washington's service and goes on
to command his own unit in the Battle of Yorktown.

1782
Hamilton studies law and becomes a member
of the Continental Congress.

1786
Hamilton calls for a Constitutional Convention to revise
the governing document, the Articles of Confederation.

1787
Hamilton begins writing *The Federalist Papers*
in support of the new U.S. Constitution.

1789
President George Washington appoints Hamilton
as secretary of the treasury.

1798
Hamilton is appointed major general of the U.S. Army.

1801
Thomas Jefferson and Aaron Burr tie in the race for president.
Hamilton advises the Federalists to support Jefferson over Burr.

JULY 11, 1804
Alexander Hamilton is shot in a duel with Aaron Burr.
Hamilton dies the next day.

GLOSSARY

ambitious—having ambition or desire for power, social standing, or fame

artillery—large guns, such as cannons or missile launchers, that require several soldiers to load, aim, and fire

circulate—to pass from person to person or place to place

delegate—a representative of a U.S. territory to a conference

economic—relating to the production, use, and sale of goods and services

foresight—seeing the future

Hessian—a German soldier hired by the British

manufacture—to make into a product suitable for use; to make from raw materials by hand or machinery

merchant—someone who buys and sells things for profit

monarchy—when a country is run by a single ruler such as a king or queen who has absolute power

policy—a course of action chosen in order to guide people making decisions; a plan embracing goals and procedures of a governmental body

poverty—the level of income below which one cannot afford to buy the things necessary to live

treason—the crime of betraying one's country by spying for another country or by helping an enemy during war

yellow fever—an infectious disease marked by aches, vomiting, fever, yellowness of the skin, and sometimes death

FURTHER READING

Quirk, Anne. *The Good Fight: The Feuds of the Founding Fathers. (And How They Shaped the Nation).* New York: Knopf, 2017.

Shea, Therese. *Alexander Hamilton: Founding Father and Treasury Secretary.* Junior Biographies. New York: Enslow, 2018.

St. George, Judith. *The Duel: The Parallel Lives of Alexander Hamilton and Aaron Burr.* New York: Speak, 2016.

SELECT BIBLIOGRAPHY

"Avalon Project: Documents in law, History and Diplomacy." Yale University. http://avalon.law.yale.edu/ Accessed October 2, 2018.

Brookhiser, Richard. *Alexander Hamilton: American.* New York: Simon & Schuster, 1999.

Chernow, Ron. *Alexander Hamilton.* New York: Penguin Press, 2004.

Federalist Papers, The. https://thefederalistpapers.org/ Accessed October 2, 2018.

Kaminski, John P. *Alexander Hamilton: From Obscurity to Greatness.* Madison, WI: Wisconsin Historical Society Press, 2016.

"New-York Historical Society, The." Alexander Hamilton. http://www.alexanderhamiltonexhibition.org/ Accessed October 2, 2018.

Randall, Willard Sterne. *Alexander Hamilton: A Life.* New York: HarperCollins, 2003.

Sylla, Richard. *Alexander Hamilton: The Illustrated Biography.* New York: Sterling, 2016.

SOURCE NOTES

p. 22, "a man of irregular..." Alexander Hamilton. Chernow, Ron. *Alexander Hamilton*. New York: Penguin Press, 2004. p. 681.

p. 24, "This is a mortal..." Alexander Hamilton. Chernow, Ron. *Alexander Hamilton*. New York: Penguin Press, 2004. p. 704.

p. 28, "I am not conscious of it..." Alexander Hamilton. Sylla, Richard. *Alexander Hamilton: The Illustrated Biography*. New York: Sterling, 2016. p. 51.

p. 29, "I am a stranger...," "I hate Congress...," and "We labor less..." Alexander Hamilton. Randall, Willard Sterne. *Alexander Hamilton: A Life*. New York: HarperCollins, 2003. p. 234 & 235.

p. 32, "the influx of..." Alexander Hamilton. Chernow, Ron. *Alexander Hamilton*. New York: Penguin Press, 2004. p. 658.

p. 32, "United States have already felt the evils..." Alexander Hamilton. *The Federalist Papers*. https://thefederalistpapers.org/current-events/alexander-hamilton-and-immigration Accessed October 2, 2018.

p. 33, "Mrs. Washington has a mottled tom-cat..." Newton, Michael E. "Tomcat Fully Refuted." https://www.slideshare.net/thepathtotyranny/alexander-hamilton-tomcat-fully-refuted Accessed October 2, 2018.

p. 36, "Arnold has betrayed..." George Washington; "a scene of the blackest treason..." Alexander Hamilton. Chernow, Ron. *Alexander Hamilton*. New York: Penguin Press, 2004. p. 141.

p. 36, "possessed of Andre's..." Alexander Hamilton. "From Alexander Hamilton to Elizabeth Schuyler, [2 October 1780]." National Archives: Founders Online. https://founders.archives.gov/documents/Hamilton/01-02-02-0884 Accessed October 2, 2018.

p. 40, "That man does not know..." Alexander Hamilton. Chernow, Ron. *Alexander Hamilton*. New York: Penguin Press, 2004. p. 508.

p. 41, "You're a scoundrel!" James Monroe; "I will meet you..." Alexander Hamilton. Chernow, Ron. *Alexander Hamilton*. New York,: Penguin Press, 2004. p. 539.

p. 43, "to which my fortune..." Alexander Hamilton. Randall, Willard Sterne. *Alexander Hamilton: A Life*. New York: HarperCollins, 2003. p. 27.

p. 44, "the larger stock of..." Alexander Hamilton. Randall, Willard Sterne. *Alexander Hamilton: A Life*. New York: HarperCollins, 2003. p. 180.

p. 45, "The people are turbulent...," Alexander Hamilton. Yates, Robert. "Notes of the Secret Debates of the Federal Convention of 1787, Taken by the Late Hon Robert Yates, Chief Justice of the State of New York, and One of the Delegates from That State to the Said Convention." Avalon Project: Yale University. http://avalon.law.yale.edu/18th_century/yates.asp Accessed October 2, 2018.

p. 50, "is not fit..." and "by far not so dangerous a man..." Alexander Hamilton. Chernow, Ron. *Alexander Hamilton*. New York: Penguin Press, 2004. p. 624 and 632.

INDEX

Adams, John, 28, 30, 33, 49–50

Alien and Sedition Acts, 30–32

André, John, 35–37

Arnold, Benedict, 34–36

Burr, Aaron, 22–24, 33, 41,
49–50

Constitutional Convention
16–19, 38, 45

Democratic-Republican Party,
32, 38, 48, 49, 50

dueling, 6, 22–24, 26, 40–41

Federalist Papers, The, 19–20,
47

Federalist Party, 32, 38, 47, 48,
49, 50

Hamilton, Alexander
birth, 7, 9
childhood, 7–10, 21, 26,
42, 43
death, 6, 22–24, 26, 40, 47
education, 9, 11
military career, 13–16,
34–37, 43
writer, 10, 12, 13, 15, 16,
19–20, 30, 36, 37, 39–40,
43, 44, 50
secretary of treasury, 7, 20,
28, 48, 51, 54–55, 57

Hamilton, Elizabeth, 24, 36,
37, 40, 44–45

Hamilton, James Sr., 8–9,
43, 45

Hamilton, Philip, 23–24

immigration, 29–32

Jefferson, Thomas, 22, 28, 32,
48, 49–50, 52, 56

Levien, Rachel Fawcett, 8–9,
21, 43

Madison, James, 19, 38, 39, 46,
48, 56

national bank, 20, 48, 52–54,
56

Philadelphia, Pennsylvania, 8,
14, 16, 18, 54

Report on Manufactures, 30,
55, 56

Revolutionary War, 6, 12–16,
27, 29, 34, 43, 52, 54

slavery, 21–22, 46–47

U.S. Constitution, 7, 18–20,
30, 46, 47

Washington, George, 11,
13–15, 18, 20, 27–29, 35–40,
42, 43, 46–49, 51, 53

Washington, Martha, 33

Washington's Farewell Address,
37, 39, 40